Finding Light in the Dark. . .

Cover designed by Carol Purkins
Author's photo by Carol Purkins

ISBN 978-1-938288-99-9

Finding Light in the Dark. . .

E.W. Purkins

Contents

*This book is dedicated to Anne Zito who
provided the impetus to a young man, with
dark thoughts and little confidence, to
release those thoughts on paper and find the light.*

*Thank you Carol for encouraging and
supporting me when darkness threatened and
my confidence wavered. You never gave up on me.*

Struggle

Feelings of guilt, feelings of fear
Attend to my mind as the end draws near.
I feel so bad when I wish him gone
And I become sick, thinking where I went wrong.

This is the way that it's to be.
Got to turn it over, set my soul free
From the bondage that's held it all of these years,
Give it to one who can handle life's fears.

Invest in a life, take a risk,
But be warned you may lose
A piece of your heart and most of your joy
As you see a life ruined by the world.

The signs are there, the end is near
For all of the selfish things held dear,
And still we cling and cast a blind eye
Ignoring the world's tortured cry.

I must follow the word, true to the end,
Not heed the voice of family and friend.
Are they any less flawed than imperfect me?
No, in my own life, their failures they see.

What conflict, his world and mine.
The glitter of this life has long lost its shine.
To look forward in absolute trust—
I fail to, but keep trying I must.

Peace

Thank God for my mind and
A chance to escape in it,
To imagine myself in white sand
Looking up at a crystal blue sky.

People in my life come and go,
And one day I'll be gone too.
It gives me great peace to know
Who will greet me when I at last pass through.

Loss of faith, anger wins,
Re-emerging of inbred sins.
Blast to the front, shot from hell.
What pain was caused when we fell.

The faith is restored, the choice is clear.
The time to be strong is here.
The way to go up is to once be down.
That chance rarely comes around.

Grant me the strength to do what is right,
What is proper and pleasing in Your sight.
Endow with courage to face this world.
Protect me from its missiles hurled.

The wall is in sight, an end to this chapter.
Does anyone know what will come after?
Another "short story" or nothing at all?
Pass through the door, heeding life's call.

Faith

When the world's day is darkest,
The weight of guilt lies on my back.
It is then that life and all its starkness
Causes my facade to crack.

Through the wreckage of my life,
A Savior boldly striding
Promises to ease my strife
If I only seek his guiding.

I pray Christ's light infuse me,
Illuminate the way ahead
In a world of lies and agony
For which His blood was shed.

Depression

The body you work so hard to keep fit
Is destined to fail in the end.
The insightful mind, the razor sharp wit
Will fade, no longer your friend.

Tired to the bone, stung to the quick,
Which is the worse day, it's hard to pick
When events stay the same as days shuffle by.
On each of those days, a bit of me dies

To get past this endless stage
Is an all-consuming hope,
The misery that is mine for this age
As for the light I grope.

What Is It About?

Mind is not here these days,
Life in a tangled maze
Lost in the cobwebs of age
Approaching the final stage.

Peace unsearchable,
What we seek.
Comfort desirable,
We are so weak.

Waiting for the Son
To appear, and all is done.
Life forever, peace,
All sin and evil cease.

What to do with what remains?
Where is time best spent?
Enough to make a man insane
Until the life is spent.

Did I take the right step?
All confidence has left.
Too late now, I've leapt.
Time will hold my fate

Fleeting life so short,
Gone in a flash of light.
No time our thoughts to sort,
Then off into the night.

Decisions seem so big right now,
But in time they shrink to nothing.
I sit and wonder why and how,
Then it's gone on forgotten wing.

The Flight

Down the highway, a figure strode.
Barren and stark it was.
Unencumbered by any load,
As free as the night wind from the north.

Casting aside for a time the weight
That bore it into hell,
Tending those it could not sate,
Forgotten in freedom's flight.

The naked life it dreamed and sought,
Stripped of all it had,
Voiding that which burdens wrought
Alone with its bare soul.

Alone indeed, a state of mind
Many search for.
None can find,
Never was nor can be.

For by the north wind borne
Blows another's burdens.
Souls, lost and forlorn
Crushing in on the mind of it.

No escape can there be,
The webs that snared it.
It cannot be free.
They extend onward, as forever.

It slowly turns back up that road
Accepting its fate.
Bending now to retrieve its load,
The physical journey at an end.

In its mind, it travels still
From stop to stop,
Never ceasing, never will,
The odyssey that is its life.

Destined to be with other ones,
To share their being,
Share their life's ruins.
This is the purpose for it and all.

Used

Are you going to fight a war?
Some will go today
Into that place, neither heaven or hell.
For some, there will be no tomorrow.

Upon the high, gallant captains
Lead their men to battle.
Some return, some do not.
The price of freedom is painfully wrought.

The ways of a few imposed on the masses,
One reason for the fight.
Kill, maim, injure, burn to ashes.
The young person's story is brought to light.

Landing in a foreign land
Half a world apart,
Faced with fears of unknown terrors,
Can you face or will you run?

Flee to nowhere, race there now.
Run for cover, run and cow.
Race to hide, sheep like men.
Hide and never show again.

A disgrace you are, never return.
To appear would subject you to scorn.
Stay away from decent folks.
Never return to your leader's yolks.

You are indeed the scum of men,
Straying from the well-worn path,
Not entitled to be free.
You must be watched until the last.

No worse a person than a coward
Does on this earth tread.
Just ask those who sit in power,
The ones who let you get shot dead.

Decision

Stuck in the center, nowhere to go.
Forward or backward, the feeling is so.
Return to the old way, safe and secure,
Travel the new road blind and unsure.

To make a decision, follow its course.
Never look back with regret or remorse.
Life only gives what you want to take.
You are only what you yourself make.

Cast away crutches, walk alone
Down cluttered pathways, the road never shown.
One day has passed, another has come,
A day with meaning, a day with none.

That day is gone, erased by the clock.
Another is coming for you to unlock.
Each passing day like opening a door.
What lies inside, your thoughts to assure.

A life such as this you want to live,
But to your fate you must yourself give.
A small part of time for study and thought
Of the goodness or waste which you have wrought.

Uncertainty

Another test will it be passed.
One more worry on a crowded mind
Isn't the first, won't be the last.
On life's trail, we wind and wind.

What a world full of pain.
What a life, devoid of gain.
What a blessing faith must be.
What a tragedy it eludes me.

Looking into a human mirror,
I don't like the image I see.
In my heart lurks a growing terror.
That man looks a lot like me.

The loss of conscience means the end
Of long-time guidance from a friend.
Now left unbridled, evil things
The mind with depraved music sings.

Cut to the heart by God's laser,
His word healing the scar tissue of sin.
Better to learn now instead of later,
My eternal victory to win.

Why

What has been gained by my life?
What benefit from worry and strife?
Is the world better for my having been
Or have I detracted by continuing sin?

Down, up—it's all the same,
Growing tired of worldly games,
Looking for a place to rest,
Comfortable, protected nest.

I should be thankful.
Why am I not?
I fret and fume,
Don't know what I've got.

In my mind, leaking to soul,
Friend after friend going to their hole.
So what do all of our vain strivings mean?
Here we are, to soon leave the scene.

Thank God He is with me
In all that I face,
Filling the empty, hopeless space
I look into my heart and see.

Tests will come and go.
I will never know.
The result is in doubt,
So I skulk, lost, about.

Watch your back, who has it?
Prepare for attack, keep your wits,
Feeling pressure from all sides,
Waiting for the knife that slides.

Man's State

Turn away from wrathful faces.
Imagine myself in other places,
Far from the tunnel vision of hate,
In a blessed, peaceful state.

Another long day of frustration
Full of indifference and spite.
Gone is the first elation
When I learned of the light.

Fading away, the things that are now,
That seem so important for us,
Soon to be forgotten scars
Torn open to remind us they are there.

Blocks in the road, holes in the way,
Encountered as we face the day.
Son above, evil on earth,
I hope He is here, giving me worth.

Can you feel the hate in the air,
The foulness of man's schemes?
Stand up for right if you dare
And live out God's gift of dreams.

Human Condition

I'm not surprised at man's ways.
Actions prove men are fools.
It's all the same, day after day,
Selling his lies with his evil tools.

Assurance found in His word
Often read, never heard,
In time of need found right there,
Inspired by the one who takes my care.

Whatever the course this life might take,
Plans broken for another's sake,
In the end all will be well.
I can't see it now but I can tell.

Pressure mounts another time.
Worry crowds the day.
Lives forever intertwined.
What a price we pay.

Face the enemy man to man.
Stop bowing, accepting his plan.
Rise up for what you know to be right.
Don't give up honor's long fight.

Side to side and all about,
The onslaught from every direction
Full of pensive, weighty doubt
Can't see the lights' inflection.

Down all the days,
Single soldiers in file
March through the maze,
Die, fall in a pile.

Folly

How can a life become this way?
No actions to take, no words you could say.
Just shake your head and wonder why,
Hoping God hears your inner cry.

The mists of age cloud the mind,
The affliction of all mankind,
Struggling to recall events,
The vigor of youth, long ago spent.

Power is what men crave
In the face of it, others cave.
Fear rules where strength fails.
In the end, man's power pales.

The hopelessness heard in the voice,
Victim of a self-made choice,
Trapped in a web of wrong.
How long?

Futility of my own aims,
Wary of mankind's games,
No secure ground in this place,
Egos prove human disgrace.

What should I write this day?
Can it be conceived in truth?
No matter what I say,
The world will try to crush.

Discontent, injustice, anger, fear
Lurking about, assaulting your ear.
How quickly we forget who is in charge,
So our trials and sins loom large.

Prayer

Distrust well founded—
I'm not exempt.
Fears well grounded
Of man's contempt.

No more talk of myself.
Cease the self-centered mantra.
Put me back on the shelf,
And think of God and this world.

The days file by
Fast or slow.
Do I want to grow old
Or just to go?

The planet decays because of men
Mindlessly pursuing their selfish end,
Casting aside all in their path.
In the end they incur the Master's wrath.

Inside all boils,
Outside appears calm.
Mind endlessly roils,
Searching for a peaceful balm.

Trouble deep within my soul.
Outside the time eternally rolls.
I see a life thrown away.
All I can do is trust and pray.

Looking into that face,
I pray for God's grace
To rebuild and renew a child,
Bringing him back from the wild.

Truth

I vow each day to still my anger,
Keep bitter words inside,
And every day they resurface,
The shame I cannot hide.

I don't want to leave Earth's stage.
I neither want to stay.
What is on the next page
In this misery play?

Lost lives, gone all wrong,
They follow sin's siren song.
And then time has passed them by,
Young to old in the blink of an eye.

No idea what this day brings.
Many times I wish I had wings
To fly away to a better place,
Escape this unending, losing race.

Dark morning inside and out.
What will this dawn bring about?
Peace and quiet, one can hope,
Climbing the eternal slope.

Forgiveness is the hardest thing
Even though I am forgiven.
I can hear His words ring,
But what of the life I'm living?

Haunting faces crowd my mind,
Cannot but the visages behind.
They will plague me into the grave.
I ask God, who alone can save.

Life in a Bag

Remnants of a life once full of dreams,
Letters full of lies and selfish ambition,
A few pieces of clothing worn out at the seams,
A pitiable human condition.

All that remains are a few precious visions,
A time growing further away,
Dimming with the passing of time and ill-made decisions,
Loss of what to think or say.

A sad small closet is all that remains,
A few old photos that bring a tear.
Of hope there is but a very few grains,
A bag of things and a future unclear.

Is this the plan? is this the path,
Causing such angst and despair?
What caused such incredible wrath
And dealt out such worry and wear?

Hope

The winds of war sweep the world.
Depraved man has seen to that.
Into death, humans hurled.
Into peace's face, they spit.

Will mankind ever learn?
I think not.
Everything will burn.
That is our lot.

Why do we hate and make war?
What is this force in our heart?
Ruin lives and homes, what for?
Such a deadly, wasteful art.

The ends of men are sick
In mind, soul, and heart.
Judgment will come quick,
Like a well-placed, killing dart.

The future without Him is bleak.
Never found, security we seek.
Relying on self, doomed to fail.
Against this truth, man continues to rail.

Thanks to Him who provides my peace
When the onslaughts come without cease.
Were it not for that, I would soon die
A death that passed without one cry.

Body eroding, soul downcast,
The best days of my life now past.
Can I see the one ahead?
If so, why this grinding dread?

One Day of Life

They rise, they fall and then disappear.
It is like they were never here.
A quick flash on the face of time,
Gone that fast without a sign.

Help me when I need it.
Leave me be when I am well.
The demands never cease,
My personal pitiful hell.

Praying, pleading, seeking an answer.
Then it is not what we want to hear.
Sin eroding, corrupting like cancer,
Crooked road we cannot steer.

World closing in,
Bones grow tired,
Awash in my sin,
Dampen the fire.

I let the word get into my head,
Actions taken, words that were said.
Plans and hopes fly away,
Black and white turn to gray.

Doors that I have let close,
What was behind them? God only knows.
Lost forever to see and live,
How many more chances will He give?

I see them dropping
One by one.
There is no stopping,
Here, then gone.

Lost

Faith, where do you go
When the world closes in?
Search but cannot know.
I've lost the battle again.

Confusion, chaos, and fear
Run rampant in lives today.
If we could only draw near
To the One to whom we pray.

Long-forgotten memories
Come to life again.
Buried deep once,
For a second they live.

Cannot tell where we will go,
Cannot say what will be so,
Cannot discern right from wrong,
Cannot avoid another fight.

Looking inside, I hate what I see.
What the hell is happening to me?
Lost feeling pervades every thought.
Peace of mind elusive but sought.

I feel confused.
Where do I turn?
Used and abused,
I'll never learn.

Conflict

Surprise attack from near,
Harsh words assault my ear.
Should I recoil in shock?
Just another stumbling block.

Anguish over things of life,
Can't control them but still the strife.
If only to give it to one who can
Follow the eternal, clear plan.

Keep my tongue in Your control.
Don't let this anger be extolled.
Go on to serve God, not man,
According to the Lord's command.

In the crossfire
Between world and God,
My body does tire,
Thoughts are at odds.

The spirit of youth long gone,
I look in the mirror today.
Final stanzas of this song,
Soon the tune will no longer play.

The tongue of a fool,
The devil's tool,
Can build up or destroy
Man's hope and joy.

Consumed by self, it is always me
Knowing, for sure that should not be me.
Crushed by my own ego's desire,
These are the lessons taught by a liar.

The Rock

Walk into the maelstrom unafraid
Knowing that evil plans have been laid.
Armor tightly girded about,
Victory is beyond all doubt.

The sky darkens more every day,
All the more reason to pray.
World gone insane, racked by sin.
Time is at hand to call the saints in.

Foolish words that hurt.
We know just what to say
To bring another down,
Darken someone's day.

What a peace I have found
When all seems dark and bleak.
Feet planted firmly on the ground,
No fear, in truth I speak

Sometimes I can see beneath the facade
That people erect to hide
The fear, the pain and uncertainty
That lurks somewhere inside.

Shown the road that I should take.
Give me Your wisdom for my soul's sake.
Total belief without one doubt,
That is what faith is all about.

The Lost One

I see fear in a young man's eyes
That all his brave front belies.
Uncertain future raises fears
In these forming, early years.

Gone now but for short while,
Remember the good times and smile.
Pray that those moments will again be here,
And the anger we know will disappear.

What is the value of one's life?
How much do you give to salvage a soul,
To live the loneliness that must be felt,
Praying to God that he be made whole?

I enter an empty room,
See the things left behind.
Encompassed by a sense of gloom,
I close the door and darkness fills my mind.

Path to the End

Does it ever end, this road of woe?
Crest one hill, seeking its end,
Onward the path goes.
I ask myself, do I have one friend?

Completion in sight in my mind's eye,
All paths traveled, no more to try.
Real is the view that we may let go
And send it off to weather life's blows.

The reality of living unshrouded by lies
That all is well, it is only my eyes
That behold the false fronts we erect
To create an aura of respect.

So strange to me is the way of God
The way He molds our circumstances,
The natural man thinks His methods odd.
He still loves after all our lost chances.

Those who went before, ones that on the edge,
Line is nearing the final gate, no escape.
I can hear turnstiles' ratchet sound,
Faintly still, going to the ground.

Fear approaches in the year of my life,
The world and word in constant strife
As it has been and always will be,
The cause of death for you and me.

Fate

I've all but forgotten the other one,
The always-
compliant other son.
I love them both, and it causes great pain
To know we may never commune again.

Dreams shattered like broken glass
On a landscape barren and cold.
My life as dead as winter's brown grass.
I know what it's like to grow old.

Body protests and gives much resistance
To my efforts to keep it in shape.
All is in vain, yet I keep on trying
To make it go the full distance.

Fall is here in the world and my life,
Third quadrant in the cycle's mill.
Cool winds carry death, cut like a knife.
The frost dulls growth and kills.

Absent the hand of God, we are doomed
To eternal torment, unending gloom.
Our mistakes we are doomed to repeat.
Look at history, sin's circle complete.

The Question

Does everyone live a life like mine
Crowded with doubt and fear,
A darkened room where no light shines
Wondering if God is near?

Approaching the dawn of the fiftieth year,
Youth long gone, the grave draws near.
Still assailed by fear and anguish,
Going nowhere, I sit and languish.

Will we ever learn we don't have the answers?
Flawed, we will never find the cure
To the sickness that destroys the world like a cancer.
Strife and man make illness endure.

I face tomorrow with uncertain dread.
Will all I hoped for be declared dead?
Cast forever in the pit of this world,
Fallen to the lies we all have hurled.

Quandary

Must learn to lay my angst down
Before it destroys my life.
The circle of misery continues around
Hurled missiles of anger and strife.

Do I dare trust the one who caused such pain?
Will peace in his actions I find once again?
No, I think not, the wounds are too deep.
In prayer, my family I will keep.

Load of guilt, will it ever be eased?
In myself, can I ever be pleased?
Is someone there to share my load?
Am I man enough to take help when bestowed?

Dreams seem so elusive and distant,
The path to them strewn with blocks.
I need to realize they may be unfulfilled.
I am crushed, yes, but one day will rise.

Erosion of Soul

There can be no rest within on my own.
Words have been spoken, the way clearly shown.
Can't seem to follow or to obey,
So in this mire of despair I will stay.

Now the other is in a time of doubt.
This is what my life is about.
Worry to worry, day after day,
As the spark of my soul ebbs away.

How can I serve, what good would be done?
It seems my own home I can't run.
I guess the decision is not up to me.
Can I let go and finally be free?

Reflecting back on what has come to pass
From the world's view, this year has been worse.
Soul stuck in this human morass,
Knowing the truth, mankind is cursed.

No cute rhymes, just a word,
Expressions of futility, frustration,
My only peace comes from God
Who will judge all the egos found unjust .

Trust again broken, another step down,
Death of a family, reason to frown.
Better yet, a cause to cry.
The ties that bind us wither and die.

The empty plains beckon to my soul.
Devoid of man, what a thought.
I cower alone in my fear-filled hole.
This is the life man's sickness has bought.

The Answer

There is little hope in this present life.
Every day down, crushed by strife
Caused by an insatiable lust for power.
Can I stand fast till the judging hour?

Clouds fill the air and my view.
On the horizon, storms start to brew.
As with nature, it is with my soul.
The storms erode, can't make myself whole.

When will I learn? How many slaps does it take
To absorb the fact, to correct a mistake?
The world will instruct, and it will be hard
To feel your dream pierced by life's shard.

I can't seem to reach him,
To break through his shell.
His chances seem slim.
Will God save him from hell?

Like a disease, the world's sickness spreads.
No hope for those sickened by this plague,
Leaving death and despair wherever it treads,
No counsel heeded no matter how we beg.

Where did life go, or was it the joy?
Whatever it was, did something destroy
The inward spark and dampen all hope,
Hanging me slowly with despair's taut rope.

Thank you, Lord, for helping me know
Where to look, where to go
To save a soul that is His to gain,
To see through and understand our pain.

Summation

The hurt and anger returned today.
I don't know what more I can say.
It has become a part of my being,
No way out within my seeing.

Over and over, the grinding goes.
Not much of me left,
God only knows.
Of faith in man, I am bereft.

Don't have a clue what tomorrow brings.
Maybe I will earn my wings
And fly far away from these earthly bonds.
Until such a time, I'll trudge along.

www.ingramcontent.com/pod-product-compliance
Lightning Source LLC
Chambersburg PA
CBHW071448040426
42445CB00012BA/1484